EXPLORING THE STATES

New Mexico

THE LAND OF ENCHANTMENT

by Christina Leaf

BELLWETHER MEDIA • MINNEAPOLIS, MN

Note to Librarians, Teachers, and Parents:

Blastoff! Readers are carefully developed by literacy experts and combine standards-based content with developmentally appropriate text.

Level 1 provides the most support through repetition of high-frequency words, light text, predictable sentence patterns, and strong visual support.

Level 2 offers early readers a bit more challenge through varied simple sentences, increased text load, and less repetition of high-frequency words.

Level 3 advances early-fluent readers toward fluency through increased text and concept load, less reliance on visuals, longer sentences, and more literary language.

Level 4 builds reading stamina by providing more text per page, increased use of punctuation, greater variation in sentence patterns, and increasingly challenging vocabulary.

Level 5 encourages children to move from "learning to read" to "reading to learn" by providing even more text, varied writing styles, and less familiar topics.

Whichever book is right for your reader, Blastoff! Readers are the perfect books to build confidence and encourage a love of reading that will last a lifetime!

This edition first published in 2014 by Bellwether Media, Inc.

No part of this publication may be reproduced in whole or in part without written permission of the publisher. For information regarding permission, write to Bellwether Media, Inc., Attention: Permissions Department, 5357 Penn Avenue South, Minneapolis, MN 55419.

Library of Congress Cataloging-in-Publication Data

Leaf, Christina.
New Mexico / by Christina Leaf.
    pages cm. – (Blastoff! readers. Exploring the states)
Includes bibliographical references and index.
Summary: "Developed by literacy experts for students in grades three through seven, this book introduces young readers to the geography and culture of New Mexico"–Provided by publisher.
ISBN 978-1-62617-030-8 (hardcover : alk. paper)
1. New Mexico–Juvenile literature. I. Title.
F796.3.L43 2014
978.9–dc23
                                                                                2013006842

Printed in the United States of America, North Mankato, MN.

Table of Contents
Contents

Where Is New Mexico?

New Mexico is a boxy state in the southwestern United States. It is one of four states that border Mexico. Arizona is New Mexico's western neighbor. Texas touches the state in the south and east. A tiny section of Oklahoma meets the northeast corner. To the north lies Colorado.

The Rio Grande snakes through the center of the state. New Mexico's capital, Santa Fe, lies in one of the river valleys. Also on the banks of the river is the state's largest city, Albuquerque.

Did you know?

At Four Corners, the corners of four states touch. People can stand in Colorado, Utah, Arizona, and New Mexico at the same time!

Utah
Colorado
Arizona
Oklahoma
Santa Fe
Rio Rancho
Albuquerque
New Mexico
Rio Grande
White Sands
National Monument
Las Cruces
Texas
Mexico

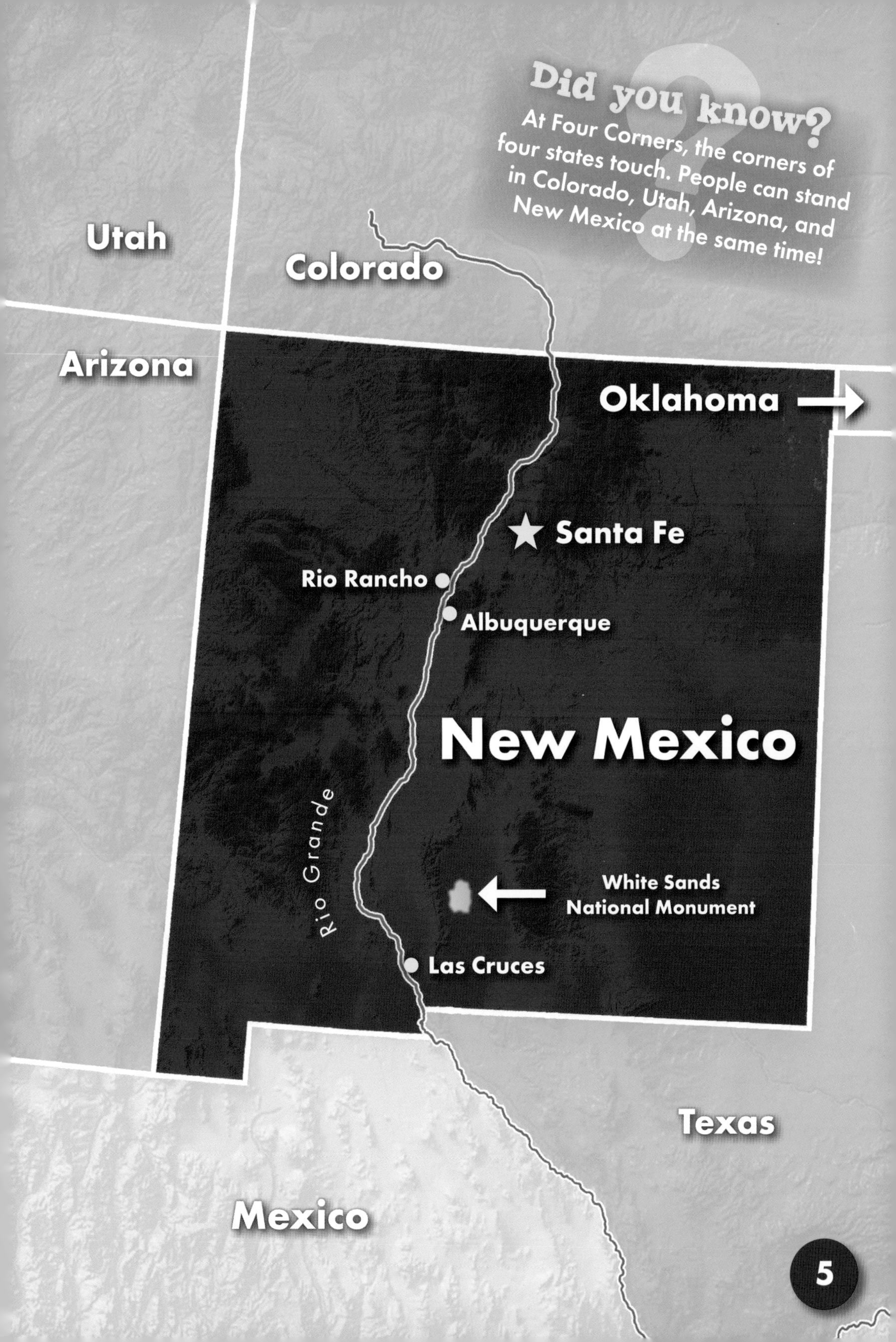

History

Native peoples have lived in New Mexico for more than 10,000 years. **Ancestors** of the Pueblo people settled in the area 2,000 years ago. The Navajo and Apache arrived from western Canada in the late 1400s. In 1540, Spanish explorer Francisco Vásquez de Coronado entered New Mexico. He had heard tales about cities made of gold. Later, Mexico took the area from Spain. The U.S. gained the land after the Mexican-American War. New Mexico became a state in 1912.

Native Pueblo

New Mexico Timeline!

1540: Spaniard Francisco Vásquez de Coronado searches for cities of gold in what is now New Mexico.

1610: Santa Fe is founded by a Spanish governor.

1821: New Mexico becomes part of Mexico.

1848: The U.S. wins the Mexican-American War and takes control of the area.

1881: Famous outlaw Billy the Kid is killed at Fort Sumner.

1886: U.S. wars with the Apache tribe end when Chief Geronimo surrenders.

1912: New Mexico becomes the forty-seventh state.

1945: The world's first atomic bomb is tested near Alamogordo.

1947: A UFO is believed to crash near Roswell.

Billy the Kid

Francisco Vásquez de Coronado

Mexican-American War

The Land

New Mexico's Climate

average °F

spring
Low: 41°
High: 72°

summer
Low: 62°
High: 90°

fall
Low: 43°
High: 71°

winter
Low: 25°
High: 52°

Chihuahuan Desert

Did you know?

In deserts, day and night temperatures can differ greatly. The Chihuahuan Desert can drop from 100 degrees Fahrenheit (38 degrees Celsius) to below freezing in one day!

New Mexico is a land of contrasts. Deep **canyons** cut through the Colorado **Plateau** in the northwestern part of the state. **Mesas** rise from the land. The **Basin** and Range region in the southwest contains mountains and deep, dry valleys. The Chihuahuan Desert reaches from Mexico into the southern part of the state.

Grassy hills of the **Great Plains** blanket eastern New Mexico. The forested peaks of the Rocky Mountains cut into the north. The whole state is usually warm, dry, and full of sunshine. However, the mountains can get cold and snowy.

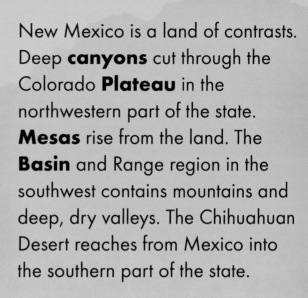

Jemez Mountain hot spring

fun fact

Hot springs bubble up from the ground all over the state. People enjoy soaking in these natural pools of warm water.

9

White Sands

Hiding in New Mexico's rocky brown deserts is a field of soft white **dunes**. White Sands is the largest **gypsum** dune field in the world. The National Monument covers 115 square miles (298 square kilometers). West of the dunes, Lake Lucero collects small pools of rainwater. When the water dries up, tiny grains of gypsum are left behind. The wind sweeps them up and forms rolling dunes.

Gypsum is a clear and shiny **mineral**. Reflected light makes gypsum grains look white. Gypsum dunes are rare because the mineral **dissolves** in water. New Mexico's dry climate is perfect for this natural wonder. Visitors can build white sandcastles or take hikes in the unique landscape.

Did you know?

The appearance of White Sands is always changing. Winds blow the sand dunes up to 30 feet (9 meters) per year.

Wildlife

mule deer

Despite the lack of water, the deserts of New Mexico are full of life. Roadrunners and mule deer speed across the land. Jackrabbits munch on cactuses while they look out for coyotes and golden eagles. **Venomous** spiders such as tarantulas and black widows scurry on the sand.

jackrabbit

mountain lion

bighorn sheep

In the mountains, bighorn sheep scramble up rocky slopes. Mountain lions prowl through forests of spruce and fir trees. Small animals such as prairie dogs and burrowing owls make their homes on the grassy plains. The twisted piñon pine grows comfortably in deserts and mountains. Spiky yucca plants are found all over the state.

Carlsbad Caverns National Park

Did you know?

Route 66 is possibly the most famous U.S. Highway. Thousands of people took this road through New Mexico on their way from Chicago to California. Though no longer used, it still represents the American tradition of traveling west.

Visitors to New Mexico explore huge underground caves at Carlsbad Caverns National Park. At dusk, people watch bats stream out of the caves in search of food. Alien hunters search for answers in Roswell. The International **UFO** Museum explores the 1947 UFO crash outside the town.

New Mexico has an abundance of *pueblos*, or ancient Native American communities. Their old apartment-like buildings are made of **adobe** bricks and can be several stories high. **Tourists** peek into daily life at a 900-year-old community called Acoma Pueblo. Others trek to Chaco Canyon. These **ruins** show how advanced early Puebloans were.

adobe homes

fun fact

The Pueblo people get their name from the Spanish word for "town." Explorers used it to describe the adobe homes. It was later used to describe the people.

15

Santa Fe

Santa Fe is known for its mix of cultures. The Spanish built it on the ruins of a former Pueblo town in 1610. Later, it was the capital of a Mexican **province**. Now it is the oldest state capital in the United States. This long and colorful history gives the city its rich culture.

There is a reason Santa Fe is called "The City Different." Instead of a skyline of towering skyscrapers, there are short adobe buildings. The people of Santa Fe enjoy a variety of cultural activities. Some watch groups perform the proud and rhythmic *flamenco*. This Spanish song and dance is characterized by strong emotion and lively expression. Others attend the opera or visit the Museum of International Folk Art.

Museum of International Folk Art

Did you know?

Santa Fe is the highest capital city in the United States. It sits 6,996 feet (2,132 meters) above sea level!

17

Most New Mexicans have **service jobs**. Some work at banks, government centers, or military bases. Others serve tourists at hotels, restaurants, and ski resorts. New technology provides many jobs in the state. Workers research **nuclear** weapons and energy. They also make computers and other electronics.

Mining is important in New Mexico. Natural gas, oil, and coal are found deep underground. Even with limited water, farmers grow hay, chile peppers, and pecans. Ranchers tend herds of cattle and sheep across the state.

Where People Work in New Mexico

government
19%

farming and
natural resources
5%

manufacturing
4%

services
72%

Playing

rafting on
the Rio Grande

New Mexicans love to be outdoors in every season. The mountains attract skiers and snowboarders in winter. During warmer months, they offer beautiful views for hikers, bikers, and horseback riders. Summer adventures include rafting down the Rio Grande. In the fall, bird-watchers keep a lookout for **migrating** birds such as sandhill cranes.

Art lovers browse the state's hundreds of art galleries. Native American ruins draw history fans. When they need a break, New Mexicans head to one of the state's many spas. They soak in warm tubs or relax with massages.

sandboarding

fun fact

New Mexicans don't need snow to go sliding down hills. Sledding and sandboarding are popular activities at the White Sands dunes.

Guacamole

Ingredients:

3 avocados, peeled, pitted, and mashed

1 lime, juiced

1 teaspoon sea salt

1/2 cup diced onion

3 tablespoons chopped fresh cilantro

2 roma tomatoes, diced

1 teaspoon minced garlic

1 pinch cayenne pepper (optional)

Directions:

1. Mash together avocados, lime juice, and salt in a medium bowl.

2. Mix in onion, cilantro, tomatoes, and garlic.

3. Stir in cayenne pepper.

4. Refrigerate 1 hour, or serve immediately with tortilla chips.

avocados

enchiladas

Green chiles are everywhere in New Mexican dishes. Hungry travelers of the famous Route 66 find them on cheeseburgers at local diners. The spicy peppers are also common in sauces, stews, and even ice cream!

Mexican and Spanish foods are popular in New Mexico. Enchiladas and guacamole can be found on many dinner tables. Puffy *sopapillas* are enjoyed in different ways. Sometimes they are served plain. For main dishes, cooks fill the fried dough with beans or meat. Bakers drizzle them with honey for dessert.

Festivals

New Mexicans love to celebrate. Native Americans welcome visitors on their many feast days throughout the year. These ceremonies honor their language and culture. Many towns remember their Spanish past with parties called *fiestas*. The Fiesta de Santa Fe is one of the oldest. It began over 300 years ago.

A different type of fiesta comes to Albuquerque each October. The International Balloon Fiesta is said to be the most photographed event on Earth. People watch as more than 500 hot air balloons color the sky. Believers and **skeptics** come together in Roswell for the UFO Festival every summer. Alien-themed events include a costume contest for people and pets!

fun fact

The Great American Duck Race is a fun August event in Deming. Competing birds flap down lanes of grass or water.

The Great American Duck Race

International Balloon Fiesta

Southwestern Art

New Mexico Museum of Art

fun fact !

Native New Mexican tribes each have their own design for artwork. They use this pattern to identify their work.

The spectacular beauty of New Mexico has inspired generations of artists. The first native peoples created decorated **ceramics**. The Pueblo wove strong baskets. Spanish folk art celebrated religion with colorful carved images of the Virgin Mary. Today, people love to buy Native American pottery, silver, and other pieces.

Did you know?
Canyon Road in Santa Fe is just three-quarters of a mile (1.2 kilometers) long. Yet it boasts more than 100 art galleries!

Taos Pueblo clay pot

Georgia O'Keeffe

Modern art also thrives in New Mexico. Georgia O'Keeffe was known for her brilliant red and yellow paintings of the state's deserts. The New Mexico Museum of Art in Santa Fe showcases her pieces along with many more. Other galleries are filled with works from new artists. Art is just one way New Mexicans express the lively culture and stunning landscapes of their state.

Fast Facts About New Mexico

New Mexico's Flag

The New Mexico flag is bright yellow. A red circle is in the center. Four groups of lines extend from the circle in each direction. This is the Pueblo symbol for the sun. The colors represent Queen Isabella of Spain, who sent explorers to New Mexico.

State Flower
yucca flower

State Nickname:	The Land of Enchantment
State Motto:	*Crescit Eundo;* "It Grows As It Goes"
Year of Statehood:	1912
Capital City:	Santa Fe
Other Major Cities:	Albuquerque, Las Cruces, Rio Rancho
Population:	2,059,179 (2010)
Area:	121,590 square miles (314,917 square kilometers); New Mexico is the 5th largest state.
Major Industries:	mining, technology, farming, tourism
Natural Resources:	natural gas, oil, coal, copper
State Government:	70 representatives; 42 senators
Federal Government:	3 representatives; 2 senators
Electoral Votes:	5

State Animal
black bear

State Bird
roadrunner

29

Glossary

adobe—a building material made of clay and straw that is dried in the sun

ancestors—relatives who lived long ago

basin—an area of land that lies lower than the surrounding land

canyons—narrow river valleys with steep, tall sides

ceramics—clay pottery that is baked in a special oven

dissolves—mixes with a liquid so that the result is a liquid that is the same throughout

dunes—hills of sand

Great Plains—a region of flat or gently rolling land in the central United States; the Great Plains stretch over about one-third of the country.

gypsum—a colorless mineral that forms in crystals

mesas—wide hills with steep sides and flat tops

migrating—traveling from one place to another, often with the seasons

mineral—a natural substance found in the earth

native—originally from a specific place

nuclear—relating to a powerful physical reaction; nuclear energy is used in certain weapons and to produce electricity.

plateau—an area of flat, raised land

province—an area within a country; provinces follow all the laws of the country and make some of their own laws.

ruins—the physical remains of a human-made structure

service jobs—jobs that perform tasks for people or businesses

skeptics—people who question the truth of a claim

tourists—people who travel to visit another place

UFO—an unidentified flying object; UFOs are often associated with aliens.

venomous—producing a poison that can harm or kill

To Learn More

AT THE LIBRARY

Craats, Rennay. *New Mexico: The Land of Enchantment*. New York, N.Y.: Weigl, 2012.

Cunningham, Kevin, and Peter Benoit. *The Pueblo*. New York, N.Y.: Children's Press, 2011.

Wencel, Dave. *UFOs*. Minneapolis, Minn.: Bellwether Media, 2011.

ON THE WEB

Learning more about New Mexico is as easy as 1, 2, 3.

1. Go to www.factsurfer.com.

2. Enter "New Mexico" into the search box.

3. Click the "Surf" button and you will see a list of related Web sites.

With factsurfer.com, finding more information is just a click away.

Index

The images in this book are reproduced through the courtesy of: Erik Harrison, front cover (bottom);
(Collection)/ Prints & Photographs Division/ Library of Congress, pp. 6 (small), 7 (right); E.B & E.C. Kellogg/
Beinecke Rare Book & Manuscript Library, Yale University/ Wikipedia, p. 7 (middle); Ben Wittick/ Wikipedia,
p. 7 (right); Science Faction/ Glow Images, pp. 8-9; Pat Vasquez-Cunningham/ AP Images, p. 9 (small);
Kojihirano, pp. 10-11; Condor 36, p. 11 (small); Joe Y Jiang, pp. 12-13; Howard Sandler, p. 13 (left);
Volodymyr Burdiak, p. 13 (middle); SumikoPhoto, p. 13 (right); Doug Meek, pp. 14-15; Natalia Bratslavsky,
p. 15 (small); David Liu, pp. 16-17; John Phelan/ Wikipedia, p. 17 (small); Universal Images Group/ Super
Stock, pp. 18, 19 (left); Buddy Mays/ Alamy, p. 19 (right); Hank Shiffman, pp. 20-21; Latin Stock/ Corbis/
Glow Images, p. 21 (small); Richard Gunion, p. 22 (small); Joe Gough, p. 22; Valentyn Volkov, p. 23 (left);
Christian Draghici, p. 23 (right); Blaine Harrington/ Age Fotostock/ SuperStock, pp. 24-25; Norm Dettlaff/
AP Images, p. 24 (small); Richard Cummins/ Getty Images, pp. 26-27; Pecold, p. 27 (top); Tony Vaccaro/ Getty
Images, p. 27 (bottom); Pakmor, p. 28 (top); Iza Korwel, p. 28 (bottom); Sonya Lunsford, p. 29 (left); Critterbiz,
p. 29 (right).